All About Michael Jordan

An Inspirational Biography and Lessons of a Basketball Legend for Children, Young Adults, and Kids

By All About Books

Table of Contents

Disclaimer and Note to Readers:

This is an unofficial tribute book to Michael Jordan from a fan for a fan to support his legacy.

The information in this book has been provided for educational and entertainment purposes only.

The information contained in this book has been compiled from sources deemed reliable, and it is accurate to the best of the author's knowledge; however, the author cannot guarantee its accuracy and validity and cannot be held liable for any errors or omissions.

Upon using the information contained in this book, you agree to hold harmless the author from and against any damages, costs, and expenses, including any legal fees, potentially resulting from the application of any of the information provided by this guide. The disclaimer applies to any damages or injury caused by the use and application, whether directly or indirectly, of any advice or information presented, whether for breach of contract, tort, neglect, personal injury, criminal intent, or under any other cause of action. You agree to accept all risks of using the information presented inside this book.

The fact that an individual or organization is referred to in this document as a citation or source of information does not imply that the author or publisher endorses the information that the individual or organization provided. This is an unofficial fan tribute book and has not been approved or endorsed by the Michael Jordan or his associates.

Before You Go Any Further, Get Your Free Gift!

Thanks for checking out "All About Michael Jordan - An Inspirational Biography and Lessons of a Basketball Legend for Children, Young Adults, and Kids" – You have made a wise choice in picking up this book!

Because you're about to discover many interesting tidbits of Kobe Bryant you've never knew before!

But before you go any further, I'd like to offer you a free gift.

My Ultimate Collection of Links to Michael Jordan's YouTube Videos!

If you're a Michael Jordan fan, you'll DROOL over this!

<u>But I'll take it down if too many people claim it as it's my personal treasure</u>. Don't miss out!

Get it before it expires here:
http://allaboutbookseries.com/jordan/

Or Scan the QR Code:

Introduction & Background

The GOAT, Magic Jordan, Air Jordan, His Airness, MJ. There are many nicknames for the man named Michael Jeffrey Jordan. No nick-name does him justice. MJ is the greatest basketball player of all time and one of the greatest athletes in the history of sports. At his peak, his fame was incomprehensible. Jordan's last NBA championship, won in 1998, was viewed by *29 million people*. The following year's finals without Jordan were viewed by 16 million people. A 13 million person drop in viewership caused by one player. Fans didn't go to arenas to watch basketball, they went to watch Jordan.

Michael Jordan's fame grew because he offered so much beyond great basketball play. He was charismatic and funny while also having one of the greatest work ethics of all time. He was *obsessed* with winning, and his desire to be the best was present in all that he did. He didn't skip practices, he didn't take nights off, he never missed a workout. If you went to see MJ play, one thing was guaranteed, he was going to give 110%.

In addition to his competitive mindset, Jordan was an extremely successful businessman. The Air Jordan brand was launched by MJ and Nike in 1984. In 2018 the brand brought in 2.9 billion dollars of revenue. Signature brands and shoes were not a regular occurrence in the 1980s. By taking the plunge and creating his own shoe, Jordan paved the pathway for many of today's NBA stars to create their own shoes. The staying power of Jordan's brand speaks to his fame. Through the course of his career, he surpassed the sport he played and ended up becoming a part of American history.

Michael Jordan's Childhood

Despite his eventual rise to become one of the most famous celebrities of all time, MJ came from humble beginnings. Born in Brooklyn, New York, Jordan moved to North Carolina as a toddler. MJ's father, James R. Jordan Sr. was a former air force man who also played semi-pro baseball. After studying airplane hydraulics in Brooklyn, James Jordan and his wife Deloris decided to move their family back to Wilmington, North Carolina to flee the increasingly dangerous neighborhoods of Brooklyn, NY. Deloris Jordan is just as impressive as Michael in her own way. She has founded and led multiple charities, and currently sits as the President of the James R. Jordan foundation. She won the Clinton Global Initiative Award in 2005, and is still an active participant in giving back to her community.

James and Deloris met at a basketball game in 1954. They quickly fell in love and dated for the next three years before getting married and welcoming their first child in 1957. While Michael was the most well known of the kids, he was definitely not the only child. James and Deloris had five kids in total, three boys and two girls.

Larry Jordan, James R. Jordan Jr., and Deloris Jordan were Michael's older siblings. MJ also had a younger sister named Roslyn. We can see the origins of MJ's competitive nature if we study his childhood, namely his early experiences with racism and competitions with his brothers.

MJ grew up in a version of the United States that had even more racism than exists presently. Wilmington, North Carolina was not a progressive area and as a child, MJ experienced a lot of racism.

"At the time you had racism all over North Carolina -- all over the United States -- and it was a lot of it around here" said Jordan. "So, as a kid, it was like, this is where I don't want to be. I want to excel outside of this. So my motivation was to be something outside of Wilmington."

MJ grew up wanting to use athletics as a vehicle to get to a better life. A life where he could journey far away from Wilmington and be able to distance himself from the racism he was experiencing.

Question: How do you think experiencing racism made MJ feel and impacted his life? How would you deal with racism in your own life?

The other source of Jordan's competitiveness came from his older brother, Larry. Growing up, Larry was a better basketball player than Michael and was able to use his advantages in strength and size to best his younger sibling. Larry was also the most competitive of all his siblings.

"My brothers hated losing, but not on the same level like me, because if you beat me back then, we had to fight, and that's just the way I was." stated Larry.

Larry was also the favorite of the Jordan siblings' father, James Jordan. MJ has called the experience of his brother being his father's favorite "traumatic" and admits that it drove him to work harder than ever. While MJ and his brother Larry were fierce competitors, there was still a lot of love in their relationship.

"I don't think, from a competitive standpoint, I would be here without the confrontations with my brother," Michael said. *"When you come to blows with someone you absolutely love, that's igniting every fire within you. And I always felt like I was fighting Larry for my father's attention. ... When you're going through it, it's traumatic, because I want that. I want that approval, I want that type of confidence. So my determination got even greater to be as good if not better than my brother."*

The quote shows a window into some of the pain that MJ grew up with. His life wasn't all flowers and daisies. He experienced racism, fought his siblings for his father's attention, and went through traumatic events. Yet what made MJ special was his ability to use painful events to fuel him and help him strive for a better life. He could have decided to stay home and refuse to play when his father favored his brother Larry, or when his community favored those with a different skin color.

Instead Michael got up, worked hard, and achieved his dreams.

Question: Do you think it's okay to fight with your siblings? How can two siblings have a healthy rivalry while still loving each other?

Michael Jordan's High School & College Years

Michael Jordan played basketball, baseball, and football during his time at Laney High. During his sophomore year of high school, MJ tried out for the varsity basketball team. At the time, he was a shorter (5' 10") athlete who was known for his baseball rather than basketball play. With the team stacked with talent, the Laney High basketball coaches decided to cut MJ from the varsity squad, demoting him to JV.

MJ was embarrassed that he didn't make the varsity team. He felt as if he was better than some of the players who *had* made the team and that he deserved a spot on the roster. The day he got cut, he went home, locked himself in his room and cried.

In typical Jordan fashion, he didn't allow himself to mope around for too long. He used the fact that he hadn't made the team as motivation. He wasn't satisfied being a decent baseball and basketball player, he wanted to be the best. MJ spent the rest of the year and the summer between his sophomore and junior years of high school working out like crazy. He worked on his game and got himself into great shape.

"Whenever I was working out and got tired and figured I ought to stop, I'd close my eyes and see that list in the locker room without my name on it," Jordan would explain. *"That usually got me going again"*.

Jordan returned to tryouts his junior year on a mission. He'd grown six inches over the summer and worked on his game every day. He made the varsity team and was instantly the team's best player, averaging over 20 points per game. Jordan didn't stop working hard just because he'd secured a spot on the team. Instead, he continued to grow his skills and dominated his junior year of basketball. MJ averaged 25 points, 12 rebounds, and 5 assists over the last two years of his high school career. He attended the Howard

Garfinkel Five-Star Basketball Camp where he showed off his game against the other top high school players in the country. During MJ's senior year of high school he would be selected to the McDonald's All-American Team due to his great performance. With his play dazzling coaches, Jordan was recruited to a legendary basketball school, the University of North Carolina.

Question: How would you feel if you got cut from a sports team like MJ did? What would you do after you got cut?

MJ spent 3 years at UNC, from 1981-1984, before declaring for the NBA draft. His college career was nothing to sneeze at. At UNC, MJ found himself on a team that was full of amazing players. He showed restraint and a willingness to be a team player by stepping back and scoring *less* than he could. Even at a young age, Jordan understood that no one wins alone. It's important to work well with your teammates in order to find success.

"Michael is just not the type to insist he be ahead of someone else." stated Jordan's father. *"He likes the system at Carolina and is not hung up on independent playing."*

During his freshman season, MJ averaged 13.5 points per game and the UNC Tar Heels were dominant. The Tar Heels, featuring future NBA stars Michael Jordan, James Worthy, and Sam Perkins, finished the season with a record of 32 wins and 2 losses. A month later, they found themselves in the finals of the NCAA March Madness tournament.

The finals featured the UNC Tar Heels against the Georgetown Hoyas. Georgetown had their own superstar player, center Patrick Ewing. It was during this game that MJ would have the first famous highlight of his career. The game was a back and forth affair with UNC struggling to score against Ewing's stellar defense. At half time the score was 32-31 in favor of Georgetown.

The teams went back and forth during the second half with the largest lead being four points by Georgetown with 12 minutes left in the game. With the game tied at 60-60, Georgetown's Eric Smith committed a foul sending UNC's Matt Doherty to the freethrow line. Doherty made the first free throw to put UNC up 61-60. With the crowd going wild, Doherty missed the second shot and Ewing grabbed the rebound. He passed ahead to Eric Smith who hit a jumper with 57 seconds left in the game to put Georgetown up 62-61.

The sequence set up Michael Jordan's heroics. Throughout his career, MJ was known for rising to the moment. When the lights were brightest, when the crowd was loudest, when the pressure was highest, MJ wanted the ball and *believed* he was going to make the shot. His self belief fueled his greatness.

With 15 seconds left in the game Jordan received a pass from teammate Jimmy Black and let fly a 15 foot jumper. Nothing but net. Jordan's teammates on the bench jumped for joy, and the game winning shot kicked off a long career of clutch shots for MJ. Jordan later quoted this moment as being a pivotal point in his career.

Michael Jordan's game-winner vs. Georgetown (1982) | FINAL MINUTE

http://allaboutbookseries.com/JordanGeorgetownGameWinnerShot

"You must expect great things of yourself before you can do them." - Michael Jordan

Question: How would you feel if your coach asked you to take the game winning shot in front of a big crowd? Nervous, excited, something else?

While the game winning shot during his rookie season represented the peak of Jordan's college career, he had lots of success in his sophomore and junior years as well. Jordan averaged close to 20 points across the final two years, and by the time he declared for the NBA draft, he was widely considered one of the best players in the country.

Michael Jordan's NBA Draft

Michael Jordan entered the NBA draft during the 1984-1985 season. He was considered one of the best players coming out of college along with Hakeem Olajuwon, Sam Bowie, Charles Barkley, and fellow teammate Sam Perkins.

The college stars ended up getting drafted in the following order:

Hakeem Olajuwon

Sam Bowie

Michael Jordan

Sam Perkins

Charles Barkley

During the NBA draft, college players don't get to choose which team they go to. It's up to chance. The Chicago Bulls finished the 1983-1984 season with a record of 27 wins and 55 losses, third worst in the league. When their pick rolled around, the Bulls selected Michael Jordan. MJ hadn't gotten lucky, the Bulls were known for running a highly dysfunctional organization.

What made MJ so special was that he focused on what he could control, not what he couldn't. The Bulls were a notoriously poorly run organization with no star players and a terrible culture. While MJ could have complained about being drafted to such a dysfunctional team he instead decided to make the best with what he had. When his teammates participated in less healthy activities such as drug use and partying, MJ didn't give up and declare the season hopeless. Instead, he worked hard and rose to lead the Bulls.

NBA Draft 1984 - Michael Jordan (Pick NO.3)

http://allaboutbookseries.com/JordanNBADraft1984

_____

Question: How do you make the best of a bad situation?

What do you do when you don't get exactly what you want?

MJ's Rookie Season

MJ was drafted into a chaotic Bulls organization. The pre-MJ Bulls were known as a "traveling cocaine circus". The team was into drugs, partying, and seemed to not care that much about whether they won games or not. When MJ was drafted by the Bulls, the team had missed the playoffs in seven of the previous nine seasons making them one of the seven worst teams in the league.

The Bulls were so bad that no one wanted to see them play. During a time where soccer was still not popular in America, an indoor soccer team, the Chicago Sting, attracted more fans than the Bulls. The drug-fueled culture of the Bulls was a shock to MJ, having come from a clean, buttoned-up program at UNC.

MJ spent most of his early years on his own. He didn't relate to his teammates and generally stuck to himself. He spent his spare time playing cards and watching movies. His mother was a frequent visitor at his modest townhouse. He didn't go to the club and didn't even drink alcohol at the time. It would have been easy for MJ to fall into a pattern of partying simply because it was the "cool" thing to do among his teammates. Instead he stayed focused, and began to lead his team to greater success.

Question: How would you react if you were surrounded by friends or teammates that weren't taking their jobs seriously and participating in dangerous activities?

MJ quickly established his position as the best player on the Bulls. During his third regular season game, facing off against the Milwaukee Bucks, Jordan scored 37 points and led the Bulls to a comeback victory, 116-111. MJ's dominance was immediately evident. He finished his rookie season averaging 28 points, 6.5 rebounds, and 6 assists per game. He shot 51% from the field and 85% from the line. After winning less than 30 games the year before, the Bulls went 38-44 and finished seventh in the Eastern Conference, making the playoffs. The Bulls faced the Bucks in the first round of the playoffs and lost series 3 games to 1.

MJ also made the all star game as a rookie, where he participated in the dunk contest. The 1985 dunk contest featured a showdown between a young Michael Jordan and noted high-flying dunker Dominique Wilkins. In the final round Dominique scored two perfect scores of 50, performing a massive two handed windmill dunk to seal the victory.

1985 NBA Slam Dunk Contest

http://allaboutbookseries.com/JordanNBASlamDunkContest1985

The 1985 all star game was also full of drama, launching a lifelong rivalry between MJ and Detroit Piston's guard Isiah Thomas. Thomas and the other veterans on the all star team felt as if it was unfair for MJ to be getting so much attention as a rookie. They decided to conduct a "freeze-out", refusing to pass MJ the ball during the game. The result was that Jordan finished the all-star game with 7 points on only 9 shots.

Michael Jordan Highlights (1985 All-Star Game) - 7pts, The infamous Freeze-out Game!

http://allaboutbookseries.com/Jordan1985AllStarFreezeOutGame

Michael Jordan's Coming Out Party

In Jordan's second year in the NBA he started off the season on fire again. He dropped 33 points against the Detroit Pistons during the second game of the year, and everything looked like he was on pace to have another incredible year. In the third game of the season, disaster struck as MJ broke his left foot. This was the first time in MJ's career that he'd ever been significantly hurt.

MJ was open about how sad the injury made him. *"I don't feel too well. I've never gone through anything like this before, and I don't know how to deal with it. Right now, I can cry all night and wake up tomorrow and find out what it's all about."* stated Jordan

Jordan gave more details about his injury during ESPN's documentary, "The Last Dance". *"I was devastated because I never* got hurt and I'm in a cast", Jordan stated. *"I couldn't do anything, I was anxious. I'm pretty sure I was irritable to a lot of people."*

Question: How would you feel if you got hurt and weren't able to play a sport that you loved for a year? Would you want to quit the team?

MJ would go on to miss 64 games that season, the most he missed in his entire career. He returned to the court late in the season, and led the Bulls to a record of 30-52, barely enough wins to make the playoffs. In the first round of the playoffs, the Bulls faced off against the number one seed Boston Celtics. The Celtics, led by Larry Bird had won over 60 games that year and were widely considered to be one of the greatest teams of all time. By all accounts the Bulls seemed to have no chance at winning.

No one would've blamed Jordan for having a poor series. Due to his foot injury he hadn't played that much basketball and he was facing one of the best teams of all time. His coaches, the fans, and the media all would've excused him if he'd played poorly.

But MJ never allowed himself to make an excuse. He prided himself on playing hard *every single game.* He didn't care if his team was outmatched, if they didn't have a shot at winning, or if he was coming off of an injury. He was determined to go out and give 110% effort anyways.

Michael came out of the gates like a house on fire. In game 1 he scored 49 points and shot 50% from the field, all while being guarded by all-defensive team player, Dennis Johnson. Dennis wasn't used to being scored on at will by his opposition. In the locker room after game 1 he stated, *"The good news is we beat them. Michael is never going to have another game like that again"*. Dennis had no idea what was coming next.

MJ followed up his incredible game 1 with arguably the greatest game of all time in game 2.

"That game represented so much of what is great in sport and basketball." said Celtics' player Bill Walton.

"He was hitting outside shots, driving to the hole. We had about everyone on the team guarding him. He obviously was in a zone. He kept them in the game with big basket after big basket. We couldn't stop him. We tried to shade him to help, everything. You were talking about a different type of talent." stated Larry Bird.

MJ dropped a sizzling 63 points in game 2, an all time playoffs record. He poured it on the Boston Celtics with a dazzling array of short jumpers and easy drives and finishes. His first step was blazing fast, an unstoppable weapon. As soon as a Boston defender looked up, Jordan was past him, collapsing the defense, and scoring at the rim. The Celtics tried various strategies to stop MJ throughout the game. The long arms of Kevin McHale. The staunch defense of Dennis Johnson. The hustle of Danny Ainge. None of it worked. Jordan was on a different level. It was as if all the pent up energy he had from sitting out all those games was erupting on the court.

The game was a back and forth affair going into not one, but two overtimes. In the end, Jordan's heroics weren't enough. The Celtics edged the Bulls in double overtime, and went on to complete the series sweep, winning game three 122-104.

The series ended up being short, but Jordan's game 2 put the basketball world on notice. The young sophomore had an argument for being the best player in the league.

Michael Jordan Playoffs Career High Highlights 1986 ECR1 G2 vs Celtics - 63pts! (720p 60fps)

http://allaboutbookseries.com/JordanVSCeltics63pts

The 1986-1987 NBA season, MJ's third year in the league, was known as the "golden era" of the NBA. The season featured 21 future hall of fame players including Magic Johnson, Kareem Abdul

Jabbar, Larry Bird, Michael Jordan, Julius Erving, Charles Barkley, and Hakeem Olajuwon. Among the stars, MJ still stood out. In MJ's third season he averaged 37 points, 5 rebounds, 5 assists and 3 steals per game on close to 50% shooting. MJ's 37.1 points-per-game is the fifth highest single season point-per-game average of all time, only trailing several seasons from hall of fame center Wilt Chamberlain.

With MJ playing at an ungodly level, the Bulls had their best record in several years, finishing the season at 40 wins and 42 losses and making the playoffs as an 8th seed in the Eastern Conference. In the playoffs, MJ's Bulls once again faced off against Larry Bird and the Boston Celtics. The results mirrored the 1986 playoffs with the Bulls getting swept in three games.

Jordan had now made the playoffs three times in a row only to lose in the first round.

Question: How would you feel if you were playing a game your team had no chance of winning? Would you play hard or decide the effort wasn't worth it?

The Bad Boys of Detroit

The 1987-1988 season launched a famous rivalry between the Chicago Bulls and the Detroit Pistons, and took the rivalry between Michael Jordan and Isiah Thomas to a new level. The season saw the Bulls begin to form the team that would go on to have great success. The Bulls added power forward Horace Grant and small forward Scottie Pippen in the rookie draft. Scottie Pippen would go on to become one of the 50 greatest players of all time, while Horace Grant would rise to become a 15 point per game power forward who influenced the game through his physical playstyle. As rookies, both Horace and Scottie weren't at the peak of their powers, but their presence was a sign of things to come.

Meanwhile, MJ was already close to the peak of *his* powers. Jordan followed up his 37 point-per-game effort in '86-'87 with a 35 point-per-game effort in '87-'88. He also shot an absurd 53.5% from the field, with the league average shooting percentage being 48%.

Led by Jordan, the Bulls continued to improve, finishing the season with their best record yet, 50 wins and 32 losses and making the playoffs yet again. In the first round of the playoffs the Bulls faced off against the Cleveland Cavaliers. The stakes were high as MJ was attempting to avoid losing in the first round of the playoffs for the fourth year in a row. MJ wasn't about to let that happen.

In 5 games Jordan scored 50, 55, 38, 44, and 39 points. He averaged a blistering 45.2 points per game for the series on 56% shooting. Despite MJ's heroics the series was a back and forth affair. The Bulls didn't have a second player to play Robin to MJ's Batman. The second leading scorer on the Bulls during the series was Charles Oakley averaging a measly 10.8 points per game.

The Bulls won games 1 and 2 against the Cavs behind back to back 50+ point game efforts from Jordan. On the brink of defeat, the Cavs, led by sharp-shooter Mark Price, won games 3 and 4 forcing the series into a pivotal game 5. In game 5, Jordan poured in 39 points and was aided by 24 points from rookie Scottie Pippen.

Charles Oakley also chipped in 8 points and 20 rebounds. The Bulls beat the Cavs 107-101 and advanced to the second round of the playoffs for the first time in MJ's career.

Young Michael Jordan EPIC Game 2 Full Highlights vs Cavaliers 1988 Playoffs - 55 Points! HD

http://allaboutbookseries.com/JordanVSCavaliers55pts1988

Question: Recall a time in your life that you did something you thought wasn't possible before. How did that make you feel?

In the second round of the playoffs MJ and the Bulls faced off against Isiah Thomas and the Detroit Pistons. Thomas and the rest of his teammates had seen Jordan's ability to pick defenses apart and they had no interest in being his latest conquest. To combat MJ's offensive firepower, Detroit Pistons' head coach Chuck Daly created the Jordan rules.

The Jordan rules were a set of defensive strategies that were specifically designed to stop Michael Jordan's offensive game. It was built on two main strategies, double Jordan whenever possible and play physical, *really physical*. The Pistons fouled Jordan hard every time they had the chance. The referees in the 1980s were less inclined to call fouls and tended to allow physical play to go unchallenged. The Pistons took advantage of the leniency from the refs and knocked Jordan down every chance they got.

"If Michael was at the point, we forced him left and doubled him. If he was on the left wing, we went immediately to a double team from the top. If he was on the right wing, we went to a slow double team. He could hurt you equally from either wing — hell, he could hurt you from the hot-dog stand — but we just wanted to vary the look. And if he was on the box, we doubled with a big guy."

"The other rule was, any time he went by you, you had to nail him. If he was coming off a screen, nail him. We didn't want to be

dirty — I know some people thought we were — but we had to make contact and be very physical." -- Detroit Pistons Head Coach, Chuck Daly

Jordan vs The Detroit Pistons Bad Boys (1988-1991)

http://allaboutbookseries.com/JordanVSBadBoysPistons

To the Piston's credit, the Jordan Rules worked. After torching the Cavs for 45 points a game in the previous round, Jordan was held to 27 points per game in the series against the Pistons. With Jordan not playing up to his usual standard, the Pistons beat the Bulls 4-1 and advanced to the conference finals.

Question: If you were in MJ's shoes, how would you have reacted to the Piston's fouling you? Would you have felt it was fair? Would you have continued to play hard?

Jordan had torched every team in the league up till that point and it was a revelation to see the Pistons have defensive success against him. With his loss to the Pistons, stories began to emerge from the media stating that Jordan's style of play didn't translate to winning. The media viewed him as a "score-first" guard that wasn't able to adequately get his teammates involved in the game.

The Pistons went on to make the NBA finals before losing to the eventual champions the Los Angeles Lakers.

The Bulls entered the 1989 NBA playoffs with renewed hope. They'd lost to the Pistons in the second round of the playoffs the year before, but had gone 47-35 during the regular season. Jordan was dominant as usual averaging 32 points, 8 rebounds, and 8 assists per game and Scottie Pippen took a step forward, averaging 14.4 points per game.

In the first round of the playoffs, the Bulls once again faced off against the Cleveland Cavaliers. The Cavs were again unable to stop Jordan as he went off for 40 points per game. He also had some additional support this time, as Scottie Pippen averaged 15 points and 9 rebounds for the series. The two teams split the first four games 2-2, with Jordan going off for 50 points in game 4 to force a pivotal game 5.

Game 5 would go down in the history books. The Cavs, led by a trio of 20 point scorers in Ron Harper, Mark Price, and Craig Ehlo were giving the Bulls all they could handle. Jordan was coming off of a bad game 4 where he had missed a clutch free throw that would have sent the Bulls to the next round.

MJ had extra motivation to beat the Cavs and advance to the next round because the Bulls were underdogs in the series. Even Bulls beat writers Lacy Banks, Kent McDill and Sam Smith had all picked the Cavaliers to win the series, in 3, 4, and 5 games respectively.

Before game 5 Jordan walked up to the beat writers. *"We took care of you."*, Jordan told Banks. *"We took care of you."*, he told McDill. Then he looked at Smith. *"We take care of you today."*

Hyper competitive as always, Jordan did not like being doubted by his fans and supporters. He used the whispers that his team wasn't good enough to win as fuel to fire him up. Game 5 was close down to the wire. With six seconds left in the game, the Bulls were down 1 when Jordan hit a pull-up jumper over Larry Nance to give the Bulls the lead. The Cavs then ran a flawless give and go with Craig Ehlo who laid the ball in to give the lead back to the Cavs. The layup put the cap on an incredible game for Ehlo. He had scored 15 points in the 4th quarter and 24 in the game. It was the best performance in Ehlo's playoff career, but it was about to be overshadowed by the heroics of MJ.

With the Bulls down 1 the ball got into the hands of Jordan at the top right of the key. Jordan drove into the lane all the while being tightly guarded by Ehlo. At the free throw line Jordan stopped on a dime, and jumped. Ehlo rose to contest the shot. As they both rose in the air, the crowd of 20,000 at Quicken Loans Arena in downtown Cleveland held their breath. Ehlo reached the peak of his jump and began to descend, Jordan kept rising. As Ehlo's hand fell away, Jordan released the shot. Dagger. Bulls win.

Jordan let out a scream and pumped his fist several times as he was mobbed by his teammates. The moment was forever etched in history, known simply as "The Shot".

The Shot: Michael Jordan's iconic buzzer-beater eliminates Cavs in 1989 NBA playoffs | ESPN Archives

http://allaboutbookseries.com/JordanBuzzerBeaterVSCavs1989

Question: How would you feel if you were being doubted by those around you?

The Bulls kept the momentum going in the second round, defeating Patrick Ewing and the Knicks 4-2. MJ continued his dominance, coming close to averaging a triple-double (36-9-8) on 55% shooting. Scottie Pippen also had a great series averaging 15 points on 58% from the field.

After vanquishing the Knicks the Bulls advanced to the conference finals for the first time in Jordan's career. One more series win and they'd be in the NBA finals and have a chance to win a championship.

Standing in the Bulls way was their familiar rivals, the Detroit Pistons. The Pistons once again employed the Jordan Rules when guarding MJ, and once again the defensive strategy was successful.

Jordan averaged 29 points per game during the series and shot 46% from the field. A full 5 points per game and 9% worse than his performance against the Knicks. The Pistons had big, strong players in Bill Laimbeer, John Salley, and Dennis Rodman. They were able to play physical with Jordan, knock him out of his rhythm, and slow down his offensive game. After losing to the Pistons 4-1 the year before, the Bulls had a slightly better showing this time around, losing the series 4-2.

The loss to the Pistons left MJ frustrated and beat down. His reputation as a scorer who just couldn't win had grown. The media criticized Michael, saying that while his scoring was great, his style of play just didn't translate to winning basketball. They praised Isiah Thomas who was known for choosing to score less in order to pass the ball more and get his teammates involved. To rub salt in the wound, the Detroit Pistons went on to win the NBA championship, sweeping an elderly Lakers team, 4-0. It looked like the reign of the Detroit Pistons was just starting, and the reign of Michael Jordan might never start.

Welcoming Phil Jackson

Going into the 1989-1990 season the Bulls knew they had to make a change. That change came in the form of new head coach, Phil Jackson. Jackson was a tried and true basketball veteran, having played for the Knicks where he won two NBA championships. After retiring, Jackson had coached everywhere from Puerto Rico to the Continental Basketball Association, where he won a title.

The current coach of the Bulls was Doug Collins. Collins, known for his fiery personality and on-court antics was like a runaway train. He'd scream and yell on the court, often ending the games drenched in as much sweat as his players were. Collins had experienced a modicum of success with the Bulls, leading the team to a 137-109 record during the course of his tenure.

As the 1989-1990 season kicked off, Bulls general manager Jerry Krause was looking for someone with a different temperament to lead the team. He understood that Michael Jordan was an extremely competitive, fiery individual and believed that it was necessary to have a more steady, cerebral coach to lead the team.

Phil Jackson fit Jerry Krause's needs to a T. Jackson emphasized a team-first style of play, running a passing-heavy offense known as the "Triangle". While Doug Collins would scream, yell, and storm up and down the court, Jackson remained calm and collected during games. Jackson was even known to teach meditative breathing techniques to his players.

"I discovered that when I had the players sit in silence, breathing together in sync, it helped align them on a nonverbal level far more effectively than words. One breath equals one mind." Jackson quoted.

Question: Why is it important to be calm? How can a calm state of mind help you in your life?

MJ and the Bulls hoped that the promotion of Phil Jackson to head coach would mean more success in the playoffs. Alas, in year one, it was not to be. In the 1990 NBA playoffs the Bulls once again found themselves head to head against the Detroit Pistons and Isiah Thomas in the Eastern Conference Finals. Once again, they came up short, losing the series 4-3.

It looked as if the defensive strategy employed by the Detroit Pistons against Michael Jordan was full-proof. MJ once again had a reduced impact on the game, shooting an uncharacteristically low 46% from the field. Jordan had now gone head to head against the Detroit Pistons three times in a row in the playoffs and had lost all three times. His rivalry with Isiah Thomas was beginning to look one-sided, and the media's narrative that his playstyle didn't translate to winning had only grown.

MJ had entered the league with lots of hype and was quickly regarded as one of the best players in the league. Now, 6 whole years into his career he had yet to make an NBA finals and people were beginning to wonder if MJ was overhyped.

It would have been easy for MJ to blame his situation. Blame the coaches, blame his teammates, blame his organization. After all, he was by far the best player on the team. He was scoring a lot. He was doing his part. It would have been easy for him to blame the rest of the world and decide that it wasn't his responsibility to figure out how to win.

Instead, in typical Jordan fashion, he went to work.

The First Three-Peat

In the offseason before the 1991-1992 NBA season MJ began planning. He had tried and failed to defeat the Detroit Pistons for three years running and he knew that he had to make a change in order to find success. It was incredibly humble of Jordan, widely considered the best player in the world at the time, to recognize that he needed to change to get what he wanted. Imagine being the *best in the world* at something, and still thinking that you had room to improve and grow.

Jordan recognized that the Pistons were able to have success against him due to their physical style of play. They were willing to foul him, and foul him hard. When he drove into the lane they'd knock him down. When he was playing defense they'd use pick and roll offensive plays to body-check him. The constant physical play took its toll on MJ. As he got more tired, his offensive game would slow down and he'd miss shots that he usually made.

MJ knew that in order to defeat the Pistons, he had to become stronger. He found his solution when he met strength and conditioning trainer Tim Grover. Grover had spent much of the 80s sending letters to NBA teams imploring them to allow him to personally train their athletes. No one responded until one day Grover got a call from the Bulls' athletic trainer, who told him one of their players was interested in his services. Grover showed up to a meeting, stepped through a door, and found himself face to face with Michael Jordan. Grover asked Jordan to give him 30 days to prove himself, and the rest was history.

For Michael's part he only had one message for Grover, *"You better keep up."*. Grover was ahead of his time in terms of training. He was like a walking, talking, Apple-watch. He would spend his time watching Jordan's game film and taking detailed notes, even going as far to count the individual number of steps that Jordan took each game. Grover took responsibility for Jordan's performance.

"The training programs were totally developed around that methodology. If something didn't work, I always felt it was my fault. If he missed a game-winning shot, even though I wasn't out on the basketball court, [I thought], "what could I have done better?" -- Tim Grover.

Jordan and Grover attacked the offseason of 1990 with a focus on one thing, *strength. "I was getting brutally beaten up."* Jordan stated to Sam Quinn of CBS Sports. *"And I wanted to administer pain. I wanted to start fighting back."*

Jordan began the offseason weighing 200 pounds. Under Grover's system, he put on muscle 5 pounds a time and ended the offseason weighing 215 pounds. Jordan's work ethic served him well. He was focused and attacked his new strength and conditioning program with a ferocity only he could muster.

"I would give him a certain amount of reps to do, but he would never stop at that number," stated Grover. *"If I asked for six, I knew he was gonna do 12.".*

In a way, that simple quote sums up a lot of what made MJ so successful. He gave 110% all the time, no matter the situation. He gave his all when he was playing in the finals, he gave his all in practice, he gave his all when rehabbing his broken foot, he gave his all when he was lifting weights. He gave his all, all the time. No questions asked.

The 1990-1991 season saw a version of MJ determined to use his new found strength to lead the Bulls to their first championship under his leadership. Jordan won the regular season MVP, scoring 31.5 points per game and shooting 54% from the field. Scottie Pippen, now in his third year, made a major leap forward, making his first all-star team. He averaged 18 points per game on 52% shooting from the field and evolved into the best perimeter defender in the league. With his long arms and athletic build, Pippen was a menace for opposing guards and forwards alike.

The team based system of Phil Jackson was paying off as well. The Bulls had 6 players average over 8 points per game, and MJ, Scottie, and Horace Grant all averaged over 12. The ball was moving and the Bulls were winning. They finished the season with a record of 61 wins and 20 losses.

The Bulls went into the 1991 NBA playoffs hungrier to win than ever. They swept poor Patrick Ewing and the Knicks 3-0 in the first round. They dominated Charles Barkley and the 76ers in the second round, beating them 4-1. That led to yet another showdown with the Detroit Pistons and Isiah Thomas. This was the moment of truth. Jordan was stronger than he'd ever been. The Bulls were running a new, high-powered offense under Phil Jackson. Scottie Pippen was no longer a rookie trying to get his bearings. If the Bulls lost now, they might never recover.

The previous year's series between the Bulls and Pistons had been full of drama with the Pistons narrowly edging the Bulls out 4 games to 3. This series was to have no drama. Jordan could not and would not be denied. He finished the series against the Pistons averaging 30 points per game on 54% shooting. A full 8% better than the year before. Scottie Pippen also stepped up, averaging 22 points per game on 48% shooting.

The Bulls swept the Pistons, winning the series 4-0 and sending themselves to the NBA finals. The Pistons were so embarrassed by the loss, that they left the floor before game 4 finished, neglecting to shake the hands of MJ and the Bulls. For MJ, the series win represented the fruits of many long years of hard work.

Jordan's victory against the Pistons can teach us many lessons. It can show us the power of endless preservation. Of refusing to give up in the face of adversity. Of being willing to grow and change even when you're the best.

The Bulls went on to defeat the Lakers that year in the NBA finals, giving Jordan his first NBA championship. The seminal play from the finals was a wild hand-switching layup that Jordan executed as he was running the fast break.

Michael Jordan - Famous Switch Hands Layup in 1991 Finals! (All Angles)

http://allaboutbookseries.com/JordanSwitchHandsLayup1991

Question: Why is it important to keep moving forward even when you lose?

The next year, Jordan won his second consecutive MVP award and the Bulls finished the season with a dominant record of 67 wins and 15 losses. After defeating the Knicks and Cavs in the first two rounds of the eastern conference playoffs, the Bulls found themselves face to face with the Portland Trailblazers in the NBA finals. The Blazers had their own all-star shooting-guard in Clyde Drexler. In an attempt to stir up interest in the series, the media framed the series as a showdown between MJ and Drexler, hoping to recreate the same kind of magical rivalry that had existed between Magic Johnson and Larry Bird in the 1980s. The narrative fueled Jordan. He knew he was better than Drexler and he was going to prove it. He came out in game 1, and set a playoff record by making six three pointers in the first *half* of the game, resulting in his now famous "shrug".

Throwback: Michael Jordan Full Game 1 Highlights vs Blazers 1992

NBA Finals - 39 Pts, Famous Shrug!

http://allaboutbookseries.com/JordanVSBlazers39pts

Jordan averaged 36 points per game in the finals and the Bulls won the series 4-2, netting Jordan his second straight NBA championship. There was no doubt about who the best shooting guard in the league was, it was MJ.

The 1992-1993 season started out with much of the same for MJ and the Bulls. Jordan finished the season averaging 32.6 points per game, and shot 50% from the field. Scottie Pippen chipped in 19 a game on 47% while maintaining his otherworldly defense.

The Bulls went 57-25 and Jordan finished second in the MVP voting to Charles Barkley of the Phoenix Suns. While the season started out well for MJ and the Bulls cracks in their armor were beginning to show. It's a known fact in the NBA that it's extremely difficult to win multiple championships in a row. The longer season takes a physical and mental toll on players and the Bulls were no exception. In addition to playing a lot of games MJ had to deal with several personal issues throughout the course of the season.

With his fantastic play and charismatic personality, Jordan had become mind-blowingly famous between 1984 and 1993. He was the most famous athlete in the U.S. and couldn't step outside without being mobbed by a crowd of loving fans. Jordan didn't have a life outside of basketball and hotel rooms. He couldn't go out to dinner. He couldn't go to the grocery store. He couldn't even go for a walk. He was simply too famous.

Despite their exhaustion, Jordan's will to win spurred the Bulls on. In the first round of the playoffs they faced off against the

Atlanta Hawks, led by high flying dunker Dominique Wilkins. Jordan averaged 34 points a game and the Bulls swept the Hawks. In the second round of the playoffs the Bulls met the Cavs, whom Jordan had famously hit "The Shot" against several years prior. Jordan averaged 31 points a game and the Bulls also swept the Cavs. So far, despite the Bulls collective exhaustion, their drive and talent were just too overwhelming.

In the Eastern Conference finals, the Bulls faced off against the New York Knicks, still being led by all-NBA big man Patrick Ewing. The Knicks put up more of a fight, with Ewing averaging 25 points and 11 rebounds per game, but also fell to the Bulls, 4-2.

Meanwhile, in the western conference, MVP Charles Barkley and the Suns had been slugging it out against the Lakers, the Spurs, and the Sonics. While the western conference series had been closer (with the series against the Sonics even going to seven games), Barkley managed to will his team to win.

This led to the NBA finals, featuring a showdown between Michael "Air" Jordan and Charles "The Round Mound of Rebound" Barkley. It was widely accepted that MJ was the best player in the league, but a championship win and an MVP for Barkley and the conversation could begin to flip. With the Bulls seeking their third consecutive NBA championship, no one would've blamed Jordan if he came out a little flat, or lacked some energy. The Suns and Barkley were young and hungry, biting at the chomp to win their first title.

But Jordan was different. He refused to let his team go down without giving it their all. As had become standard for his career, when the lights shone brightest, when the pressure was on, and when everyone expected him to fail, he rose.

MJ faced off against the Suns and had one of the greatest series in NBA finals history. He averaged a scorching 41 points, 9 rebounds, and 6 assists per game, all while shooting over 50% from the field. To have *one* forty point game in the finals is impressive. To average it for the entire series was mind-boggling. Charles Barkley was no pushover, averaging 27 points and 13 rebounds per game to keep the Suns in the series. The Suns guards, Kevin Johnson and Dan Majerle also played well, each scoring 17 points a game.

Barkley and the Suns quickly figured out what most of MJ's rivals did. MJ was relentless. His combination of talent, work ethic, and unbreakable determination were an impossible mountain to climb. The Bulls won the series 4-2, and Jordan had his third consecutive title. He'd come a long way since his losses to the Pistons. The championship put a cap on a seven year run for Jordan and the Bulls where MJ won 7 scoring titles and 3 championships.

Michael Jordan 42 pts,12 reb,9 ast vs Charles Barkley 42 pts,13 reb, nba-finals 93, game 2

http://allaboutbookseries.com/Jordan42ptsCharlesBarkley

Michael Jordan's First Retirement

The long journey had taken a toll on Jordan. There were signs of cracks in his seemingly unbreakable armor during the playoffs. He'd been seen gambling late into the night at an Atlantic City casino while *having a game to play the next day* and seemed uncharacteristically disengaged. To make matters worse, tragedy struck MJ and his family in July of 1993 when his father was murdered.

MJ and his father James Jordan were inseparable. MJ valued his father's advice, and James was extremely proud of the accomplishments of his son. *"He's a voice of reason that always drove and challenged me. That's the type of father I had"* said Jordan, speaking to director Jason Hehir in ESPN's documentary The Last Dance.

On July 22nd, 1993, James Jordan was spending the day in Wilmington, NC. That night he began a drive from Wilmington to

Charlotte, NC. While James was traveling, he decided to pull to the side of the road in order to catch a quick nap, rather than risking driving while sleepy. It was a highly responsible act from MJ's father, but it would lead to his demise. Two men -- Daniel Green and Larry Demery -- noticed the vehicle stopped on the side of the road and decided to take advantage of the situation. They shot James Jordan and stole his car. His body was found in a nearby swamp three weeks later.

The killing of his father was the straw that broke the camel's back for Michael. The media had begun to speculate that MJ had a gambling problem, and seeing the death of his father, unfairly linked the two events together. Article after article was written implying that MJ had a gambling problem and that the murder of his father was somehow linked to unpaid gambling debts. The stories were shown to be false.

The scrutiny and unfair criticism, in combination with the sadness over the death of his father caused MJ to break. Thus, in the year of 1993 Michael Jordan announced to the basketball world that he was retiring. He was the best player. He was the most famous athlete. He'd just won three championships in a row. And he was done.

Question: How do you think MJ felt when the media wrote stories about the death of his father?

MJ shocked the world by retiring from basketball. Imagine LeBron James retiring after beating the Warriors in 2016. Tiger Woods retiring after winning the Masters. During his brief retirement, MJ attempted to make it as a Major League Baseball player for the Chicago White Sox, signing a contract with their minor league team. Jordan said the decision was dedicated to his father who had always imagined MJ as a Major League Baseball player.

MJ's brief attempt at playing baseball has been historically viewed as a failure. MJ didn't get to play in the majors and never made it beyond double-A baseball. However, a closer look at MJ's baseball career reveals a surprising amount of success. Playing for the Birmingham Barons in double-A, Jordan hit .202, with 3 HRs, 51 RBIs, and 30 steals. MJ also played for the Scottsdale Scorpions in the Arizona Fall League hitting .252 against top competition.

What most fans don't realize is that double-A is home to the most raw talent in the minors. Major league baseball teams send their up and coming young talent to double-A, and often those players make the leap from double-A directly to the majors. The fact that Jordan was able to jump into double-A baseball and have *any* success at all is a testament to his supreme athleticism and confidence. If Jordan were to have stuck with baseball it's likely that he could've made his way to the majors at some point. But the call of basketball proved to be too strong.

Michael Jordan plays right field for the White Sox

http://allaboutbookseries.com/JordanPlaysfortheWhiteSox

Question: Talk about a time you tried out something new that you weren't good at. How did it feel? Did you stick with it or did you give it up?

After Jordan's retirement the Bulls began the 1993-1994 season without him. It isn't well known but the Bulls actually fought their way to a good record without Jordan, finishing with a 55-27 record while being led by Scottie Pippen. After sweeping the Cavs in the first round of the playoffs 3-0, the Bulls once again faced off against Patrick Ewing and the New York Knicks. With Jordan, the Bulls had defeated the Knicks several times in the playoffs, but this time things were to go differently. Ewing averaged 23 points and 12 rebounds per game for the series while shooting 53% from the field. Scottie Pippen did his best Michael Jordan impersonation averaging 22 points per game, but only managed to shoot 40%. The Knicks won the series in seven games and the Bulls were eliminated from the playoffs for the first time in four years.

The wheels really began to come off during the 1994-1995 NBA season. The Bulls found themselves with a 31-31 record 62 games into the season and in danger of missing the playoffs. They desperately needed MJ to come back. They weren't the only ones. Sports were suffering in the U.S.A. The MLB was in the middle of a strike, the National Hockey League was having a lockout, and O.J. Simpson's trial was leaving sports fans shocked and disturbed. Finally, in March of 1995, MJ used a fax machine to send a two word message that would rock the world of sports, *"I'm back."*

Despite being out of the league for over a year, Jordan's impact on the Bulls was immediate. The betting odds for the Bulls winning the title were 40-1 before Jordan's announcement and quickly shifted to 5-1 when he came back. In the time that Jordan had been away from the sport the Bulls team had changed. Scottie Pippen was still the team's star point-forward and defender, but center Bill Cartwright and long time forward Horace Grant had both departed from the team. In their place the Bulls had added sharp shooter Steve Kerr, talented offensive forward Toni Kukoc, Pete Myers, and Bill Wennington.

The year Jordan returned is often forgotten by fans and the media. The reality was that when Jordan returned the Bulls took a while to regain their previous chemistry. When the Bulls met the Orlando Magic in the 1995 playoffs, Jordan found himself staring down a young, hungry Shaq and Penny Hardaway.

Jordan had a good series against the Magic, averaging 31 points a game on 48% shooting from the field. However, the size and athleticism of Shaq proved too much for Jordan and the Bulls and the Magic won the series 4-2, eliminating the Bulls from the playoffs.

The Second Three-Peat

After losing to the Magic the previous year, Jordan and the Bulls came back with a vengeance. Bolstered by the addition of defensive player of the year candidate and elite rebounder Dennis Rodman (formerly a Detroit Piston!), the Bulls went on a winning tear that hadn't been seen in the history of basketball.

MJ was still the best player in the world at this time, an elite scorer that dominated the game on both sides of the ball. However, his game was different from his younger years. He had lost some of his explosiveness, some of his athleticism. He no longer could jump over players and instead had to find ways around them.

There's an old saying that goes "father time is undefeated" and MJ was no exception. MJ showed the true mindset of a champion by continuing to grow his game as he got older. From 1995 to 1998 Jordan no longer relied on being the most dominant athlete. Instead he worked on his footwork and shooting, becoming the most lethal mid range shooter in NBA history. Trading out acrobatic layups for turnaround jump shots, MJ showed that he was willing to learn, even after achieving enormous amounts of success.

The '95-'96 version of the Bulls went 72-10 and set the regular season record for most wins in a season. Jordan won another MVP award, but the audience could see that he was at a different point of his career. The dominance of the mid 90s, where Jordan would regularly score over 30 points per game on well over 50% shooting from the field was gone. In its place was a craftier, wiser MJ.

The 1996 NBA playoffs started with the Bulls keeping their regular season momentum going. They swept the Miami Heat in the first round with MJ averaging 30 a game on 52% shooting. In the second round they once again faced off against Patrick Ewing and the Knicks and once again were triumphant, winning the series 4-1. MJ was particularly dominant, ratcheting up his scoring to a blistering 36 points per game. Patrick Ewing was one of the greatest players of his generation, and probably would have won a championship if he hadn't had the misfortune of playing at the same time as Michael Jordan.

In the Eastern Conference finals, MJ once again found himself face to face with the Orlando Magic, led by Shaq and Penny Hardaway. This time, he would not be stopped. Jordan averaged 30 points per game on 52% shooting from the field, while Scottie Pippen averaged 18 points, 7 rebounds, and 7 assists per game. New addition Dennis Rodman also proved to be extremely valuable as he got up for an unfathomable *16* rebounds per game during the series. The Bulls swept the Magic, 4-0, and effectively broke up the team, as Shaq decided to go to the Los Angeles Lakers that summer.

In the finals, MJ found himself facing a new adversary. The Seattle SuperSonics, led by defensive legend Gary Payton and athletic force of nature Shawn Kemp. Gary Payton was nicknamed "The Glove" for his ability to steal the ball from the player he was guarding. Payton's legendary defense actually worked on MJ. For the series, Jordan only shot 42% from the floor, one of the worst marks of his career.

Despite his poor shooting performance, MJ showed that he had become wiser over the years. His constant studying of the game of basketball was about to pay off. The younger MJ who faced off against the Pistons might have tried to force the issue with Gary Payton, continuing to shoot and miss until his team had no chance to win the game. This version of MJ took his foot off the gas. He shot less and passed more. He got his teammates involved and trusted their team defense to pull them through. The strategy worked, the Bulls had 6 players score over 5 points per game and 4 players score over 10. Center Luc Longely had a particularly good series averaging 12 points a game on a high efficiency 58% from the field.

Question: Talk about the importance of teamwork. Why was it important for Jordan to pass the ball more and let his teammates handle more of the offense?

Bulls vs. Magic - 1996 Eastern Conference Finals (Game 3)

http://allaboutbookseries.com/JordanBullsVSMagic1996

The Bulls won the series 4-2 and MJ had his fourth

championship locked up.

The 96-97 version of the Bulls saw much of the same for MJ

and the Bulls. They dominated the league on their way to a record of

69-13. Jordan was still a dominant scorer, averaging close to 30 per

game, but had learned to rely a little more on his teammates. Scottie

Pippen averaged over 20 a game and Toni Kukoc averaged 13.

Despite the Bulls dominant record and Jordan's stellar

performance he lost the MVP award to Utah Jazz forward, Karl

Malone. The Jazz had risen as a contender for the title in the last few years, being led by the dominant play of Malone and point guard John Stockton. The Bulls and the Jazz seemed like they were destined to meet in the finals, and they were. Both teams blasted through their respective conferences with relative ease.

In the finals they traded blows for the first four games of the series. In game 1, Jordan scored 31 points and won the game on a buzzer beater. The Bulls also won game two on a scorching 38 points by Jordan. The Jazz came back to win games 3 and 4 as Karl Malone dominated the Bulls big men. However, it was game 5 that would go down in history.

The night before game 5, MJ and his friends were up playing cards at his hotel room. At 10:30 in the night, Jordan asked for some pizza to be delivered. The pizza was delivered to the hotel room and Jordan's trainer, Tim Grover, said he had a bad feeling about it.

"They're all trying to look in because everyone knew it was Michael. So I take the pizza, I pay them, I put this pizza down and I said 'I got a bad feeling about this.'" says Tim Grover in The Last Dance documentary on ESPN.

MJ ignored Grover's warning and ate the entire pie on his own. At 2:30 in the morning he found that he'd made a mistake as he woke up sick and began vomiting. Jordan called Grover, who found him curled up in a ball, shaking. Jordan wasn't a participant in practice the next day, instead spending the day hooked up to an IV. The Bulls athletic training staff told Jordan there was no way he could play. In typical MJ fashion, Jordan thought differently. He told coach Phil Jackson that he would play and act as a "decoy" in game 5.

The game started off poorly. Jordan was able to make his way up and down the court, but spent timeouts collapsed on the bench, a towel draped over his head. Several times his teammates had to help

MJ make his way off the court, and it looked like the Bulls were on their way to a game 5 loss. What happened next was incredible.

Jordan began to heat up. Fighting through the pain he rose time and time again to make jumpshot after jumpshot. Hitting a dazzling array of threes, transition layups, step back jumpers, and turn around fadeaways Jordan ended up torching the Jazz for *38 points*, all while being barely able to stand.

Michael Jordan "The Flu Game" Highlights 1997 Finals G5 vs Jazz - 38pts! (HD 720p 60fps)

http://allaboutbookseries.com/JordanTheFluGame1997Finals38pts

The Bulls won the game by two points and the Jazz were broken mentally. If they couldn't beat MJ when he was sick, when could they beat him? They folded in game 6 and Jordan had his fifth championship. The "flu game" as it came to be known was the ultimate testament to MJ's focus and drive. Even when his body was rebelling, his mind was so resilient that he could will himself to heights the rest of the world couldn't imagine.

Question: What do you think about the flu game? How was Jordan able to play despite being sick?

After the Bulls beat the Jazz in 1996 they seemed unstoppable. MJ had now won 5 championships and only been defeated the year he came back from his baseball retirement. It seemed like the Bulls dynasty would last forever, but it was not meant to be.

The 1997-1998 season began with drama. A rift had formed between Bulls general manager Jerry Krause and head coach Phil

Jackson. Despite the Bulls overwhelming success, Krause was determined to push Jackson out of his position as head coach. Before the season even started, Krause announced to the media that the year would be Phil Jackson's last as head coach, no matter what. Krause told Jackson, *"I don't care if it's 82 and 0 this year, you're gone."*

In typical Phil Jackson fashion, rather than giving up he found a way to inspire his team. He nicknamed the season "The Last Dance", and inspired his players to fight for one last championship.

Fighting for Jackson, the Bulls went 62 and 20 during the regular season. Jordan was showing signs of wear and tear throughout the season. He was 13 years into his career and far removed from his peak athleticism. He still scored 29 points a game and managed to shoot 47% from the field, mostly relying on his dominant mid range game.

In the 1998 NBA playoffs, the Bulls faced off against the New Jersey Nets in the first round. They made quick work of the Nets sweeping them 3-0. In the second round of the playoffs the Bulls met

the Charlotte Hornets. The Bulls made quick work of them as well,

beating them 4-1.

In the Eastern Conference finals the Bulls met a new foe, the

Indiana Pacers led by three point sharpshooter Reggie Miller. The

Pacers gave the Bulls all they could handle, but discovered what the

rest of Jordan's opponents had discovered. He was unbeatable. The

Bulls squeezed by the Pacers in seven games before meeting the Jazz

once again in the NBA finals. The Last Dance had reached its final act.

The series started off in favor of Chicago and the Bulls were

up three games to one after four. Being on the brink of elimination,

Karl Malone of the Jazz came out and had a dominant game five.

Scoring 39 points, Malone kept the Jazz's season alive and forced a

game six.

Game 6 went back and forth, back and forth. With 43 seconds

left in the game, Jazz point guard John Stockton launched a three.

Bang, the shot went down and put the Jazz up by three points with 40 seconds remaining. Jordan immediately came down the other end and drove for a layup bouncing it in high off the backboard. The Jazz lead was down to one. On the ensuing Jazz possession, Stockton got Malone the ball in the post. The Bulls double-teamed Malone and Jordan stole the ball. Jordan came down the court, drove to the freethrow line, stopped on a dime, and rose. He let the jumper fly and held the follow through. Swish.

Michael Jordan LAST Bulls Game, Game 6 Highlights vs Jazz 1998 Finals - 45 Pts, EPIC CLUTCH SHOT

http://allaboutbookseries.com/JordanLastBullsGame

Jordan's jumper put the Bulls up by 1 with 5 seconds left and clinched them yet another NBA title. It was Jordan's sixth title, his third straight, and pushed his record to 6-0 in the finals. His layup → steal → game-winner sequence to end the season remains one of the most legendary sequences of plays in sports.

Finale

Michael Jordan ended his career with a list of accomplishments that are beyond staggering. He was a:

14 time all star

10 time scoring champion

6 time NBA champion

5 time regular season MVP

6 time NBA finals MVP

11 time all-NBA team member

9 time all-defensive team member

He went up against and defeated some of the greatest basketball players of all time, and is largely responsible for several of his peers never winning an NBA championship. The list of those who tried to beat MJ and lost includes:

Patrick Ewing

Charles Barkley

Reggie Miller

Shawn Kemp

Gary Payton

Penny Hardaway

John Stockton

Karl Malone

Beyond his material accomplishments Jordan showed us what was possible with a focused mindset and unending work ethic. His career was not without obstacles. He was drafted into a highly dysfunctional organization. He went through multiple coach changes. He lost in the playoffs to his biggest rival (Isiah Thomas) three years in a row. He had to endure the personal tragedy of the murder of his father. He suffered a broken foot in his second year in the league. He got food poisoning *during* an NBA finals.

Throughout all the obstacles MJ's drive never went away. He showed up and played hard every night. He found solutions to his problems. He didn't blame his teammates or his situation, he took

the responsibility onto himself. And that's what made him legendary.

MJ's Timeline

Feb 17, 1963 → Michael Jordan is born in Brooklyn, NY

1981 → Michael Jordan decides to play college ball at the University of North Carolina

1984 → Michael Jordan declares for the NBA draft and is selected with the 3rd pick by the Chicago Bulls

1985 → Jordan wins the rookie of the year award, averaging 28.5 points per game

1986 → Jordan leads the Bulls to the playoffs despite breaking his foot and missing 64 games of the regular season

1986 → Jordan sets an NBA record by scoring 63 points against the Boston Celtics in round one of the NBA playoffs

1989 → Jordan hits "The Shot" to beat the Cleveland Cavaliers in the NBA playoffs

1991 → Jordan and the Bulls win their first championship against the Los Angeles Lakers

1992 → Jordan and the Bulls win their second championship against the Portland Trailblazers. Jordan has the famous "shrug" game.

1993 → Jordan and the Bulls win their third straight championship and defeat Charles Barkley and the Phoenix Suns in the NBA finals.

1993 → Michael Jordan's father, James Jordan is murdered. Jordan retires from basketball for the first time.

1994 → Jordan begins playing for the Chicago White Sox minor league affiliate team

1995 → Jordan returns to the NBA, and ends up losing to the Shaq led Orlando Magic in the playoffs.

1996 → Jordan and the Bulls win their fourth championship, defeating Gary Payton, Shawn Kemp, and the Seattle SuperSonics in the NBA finals.

1997 → Jordan and the Bulls defeat the Utah Jazz for the first time, securing their fifth NBA title.

1998 → Bulls general manager Jerry Krause declares that the season will be Phil Jackson's last, prompting Jackson to name the season "The Last Dance".

1998 → Jordan hits a game winning shot in game 6 of the NBA finals to secure the Bulls 6th championship, their second three-peat and his 6th NBA finals MVP.

2009 → Michael Jordan is inducted into the basketball hall of fame. He is considered the greatest basketball player of all time.

References

General | basketball-reference.com

General | espn.com

Intro | https://clutchpoints.com/the-last-dance-news-michael-jordan-added-15-pounds-of-muscle-to-match-up-vs-pistons/

Intro | https://tvbythenumbers.zap2it.com/sports/nba-finals-tv-ratings-1974-2008/

Childhood | https://www1.cbn.com/700club/what-michael-jordans-mother-knows-about-parenting

Childhood | https://www.womenshistory.org/education-resources/biographies/deloris-jordan

HS | https://www.interbasket.net/news/michael-jordans-high-school-stats-and-accomplishments/19696/

College | https://www.interbasket.net/news/michael-jordans-college-stats-and-achievements/19685/

NBA Draft |

https://www.landofbasketball.com/draft/1984_nba_draft.htm

NBA Draft | https://www.nba.com/bulls/history/flip-coin-helped-bulls-land-jordan

Early Rookie Years | https://nypost.com/2020/04/19/the-last-dance-pre-michael-jordan-bulls-were-traveling-cocaine-circus/

Early Rookie Years |

https://www.nbcsports.com/bayarea/warriors/michael-jordan-devastated-breaking-foot-vs-warriors-last-dance

Early Rookie Years |

https://www.chicagotribune.com/sports/bulls/ct-chicago-bulls-michael-jordan-ankle-injury-20200419-

5a3pynptrrf47pcm6xbmwv2q4y-story.html

Early Rookie Years | https://www.nba.com/bulls/history/michael-

jordans-63-points-1986-nba-playoffs-may-have-been-greatest-game-

ever-played.html

Pistons Roadblock |

https://www.sportingnews.com/au/nba/news/what-are-the-jordan-

rules-what-you-need-to-know-about-the-defence-the-bad-boys-

detroit-pistons-made-famous-the-last-

dance/173ecum38spgn102m2uptwuk7u

Pistons Roadblock | https://clutchpoints.com/the-last-dance-news-

how-phil-jackson-became-head-coach-of-the-bulls/

First threepeat | https://www.yahoo.com/lifestyle/michael-jordans-

trainer-tim-grover-173026998.html

First threepeat | https://clutchpoints.com/the-last-dance-news-michael-jordan-added-15-pounds-of-muscle-to-match-up-vs-pistons/

First threepeat | https://www.esquire.com/entertainment/tv/a32417623/michael-jordan-father-death-james-jordan-media-conspiracy/

Jordan's comeback | https://theundefeated.com/features/the-day-michael-jordan-announced-his-return-to-the-nba/

Second Threepeat | https://www.cbr.com/the-last-dance-reveals-truth-michael-jordan-flu-game/

Final Surprise Bonus

Final words from the author…

Hope you've enjoyed this biography of Michael Jordan.

It was an utmost privilege performing deep research and bringing forth these information to the public for you to enjoy.

I always like to overdeliver, so I'd like to give you one final bonus.

Do me a favor, if you enjoyed this book, please leave a review on Amazon.

It'll help get the word out so more people can find out more about our beloved superstar as a tribute and homage.

If you do, I'll send you one of my most cherished video collection – Free:

Take a Trip into Michael Jordan's Mind: Michael Jordan's Mind-Boggling Interviews!

You won't be able to understand Michael Jordan fully until you understand how he thinks.
As a Michael Jordan fan, you'll find this utmost valuable and cannot be missed!

Here's how to claim your free report:

1. Leave a review right away -

2. Send a screenshot of your review to:
   reviews@allaboutbookseries.com

3. Receive your free video collection – "Take a Trip into Michael Jordan's Mind: Michael Jordan's Mind-Boggling Interviews"– *immediately*!